GREEK MYTHOLOGY

FOR KIDS

LEGENDARY STORIES OF GODS, HEROES, AND MYTHOLOGICAL CREATURES

ZACHARY HAMBY

ILLUSTRATIONS BY YANCEY LABAT

ROCKRIDGE PRESS

FOR JASON

"As you set out for Ithaka, hope the voyage is a long one, full of adventure, full of discovery."

—C. P. CAVAFY

First Rockridge Press trade paperback edition 2022

Rockridge Press and the Rockridge Press logo are trademarks or registered trademarks of Callisto Media Inc. and/or its affiliates in the United States and other countries and may not be used without written permission.

For general information on our other products and services, please contact our Customer Care Department within the United States at (866) 744-2665, or outside the United States at (510) 253-0500.

Paperback ISBN: 978-1-68539-682-4 | eBook ISBN: 978-1-68539-776-0

Manufactured in the United States of America

Interior and Cover Designer: Richard Tapp
Art Producer: Janice Ackerman
Editor: Julie Haverkate
Production Editor: Melissa Edeburn
Production Manager: Martin Worthington

Illustrations © 2022 Yancey Labat
Author photo courtesy of Rachel Hamby

10 9 8 7 6 5 4 3 2 1 0

GREEK MYTHOLOGY

FOR KIDS

LEGENDARY STORIES OF GODS, HEROES, AND MYTHOLOGICAL CREATURES

ZACHARY HAMBY

ILLUSTRATIONS BY YANCEY LABAT

ROCKRIDGE PRESS

FOR JASON

"As you set out for Ithaka, hope the voyage is a long one, full of adventure, full of discovery."

—C. P. CAVAFY

First Rockridge Press trade paperback edition 2022

Rockridge Press and the Rockridge Press logo are trademarks or registered trademarks of Callisto Media Inc. and/or its affiliates in the United States and other countries and may not be used without written permission.

For general information on our other products and services, please contact our Customer Care Department within the United States at (866) 744-2665, or outside the United States at (510) 253-0500.

Paperback ISBN: 978-1-68539-682-4 | eBook ISBN: 978-1-68539-776-0

Manufactured in the United States of America

Interior and Cover Designer: Richard Tapp
Art Producer: Janice Ackerman
Editor: Julie Haverkate
Production Editor: Melissa Edeburn
Production Manager: Martin Worthington

Illustrations © 2022 Yancey Labat
Author photo courtesy of Rachel Hamby

10 9 8 7 6 5 4 3 2 1 0

THIS BOOK BELONGS TO:

....

....

CONTENTS

yths are stories that teach. The word *myth* comes from the Greek word *mythos*, which means "story of the people." Myths are a culture's special stories, passed from generation to generation, and they serve two purposes. First, they explain why the world works the way it does. Why do the seasons change? Why does a volcano erupt? Why does the sun sometimes go dark? Second, myths teach important lessons about life. Some myths show how life should be lived. Others serve as warnings against human foolishness.

Myths have never been set in stone. Today, you can often find multiple versions of the same myth because for hundreds of years myths were only told out loud, and details changed with each telling. When people finally began writing myths down, writers each chose the version they liked best. This collection retells the most well-known version of each story, but in other books, you can explore different versions.

Studying mythology helps us spot references to myths almost everywhere in the modern world. Your new Nikes (named for Nike, the Greek goddess of victory) touch your **Achilles** tendon (named for the Greek hero Achilles) on your walk to the museum (named for the Greek muses) on Saturday (named for the Roman god Saturn).

Myths also give us a glimpse into a different time and culture. Life in ancient Greece was much different than in our age. Instead of one unified country, Greece was home to many **city-states**, powerful cities that ruled the area around them like a state. When the myths were written, democracy was not a form of government. Kings and queens ruled. Everyday life was different as well. Women were not always given the same freedoms as men, and children were sometimes treated cruelly. Because the stories in this book are retellings of ancient myths, you will find certain groups of people presented differently or less frequently than they would be in modern times.

Myths inspire us to use our strengths and remind us of our weaknesses. In this book you will find stories of powerful gods and goddesses, mighty heroes, valiant warriors, terrifying monsters, and fantastic creatures; these characters fight, love, envy, succeed, and sometimes fail—just like you and me. Myths still have many lessons to teach if we are willing to listen.

of each story, but in other books, you can explore different versions.

Studying mythology helps us spot references to myths almost everywhere in the modern world. Your new Nikes (named for Nike, the Greek goddess of victory) touch your **Achilles** tendon (named for the Greek hero Achilles) on your walk to the museum (named for the Greek muses) on Saturday (named for the Roman god Saturn).

Myths also give us a glimpse into a different time and culture. Life in ancient Greece was much different than in our age. Instead of one unified country, Greece was home to many **city-states**, powerful cities that ruled the area around them like a state. When the myths were written, democracy was not a form of government. Kings and queens ruled. Everyday life was different as well. Women were not always given the same freedoms as men, and children were sometimes treated cru-elly. Because the stories in this book are retellings of ancient myths, you will find certain groups of people presented differently or less frequently than they would be in modern times.

Myths inspire us to use our strengths and remind us of our weaknesses. In this book you will find stories of powerful gods and goddesses, mighty heroes, valiant warriors, terrifying monsters, and fantastic creatures; these characters fight, love, envy, succeed, and sometimes fail—just like you and me. Myths still have many lessons to teach if we are willing to listen.

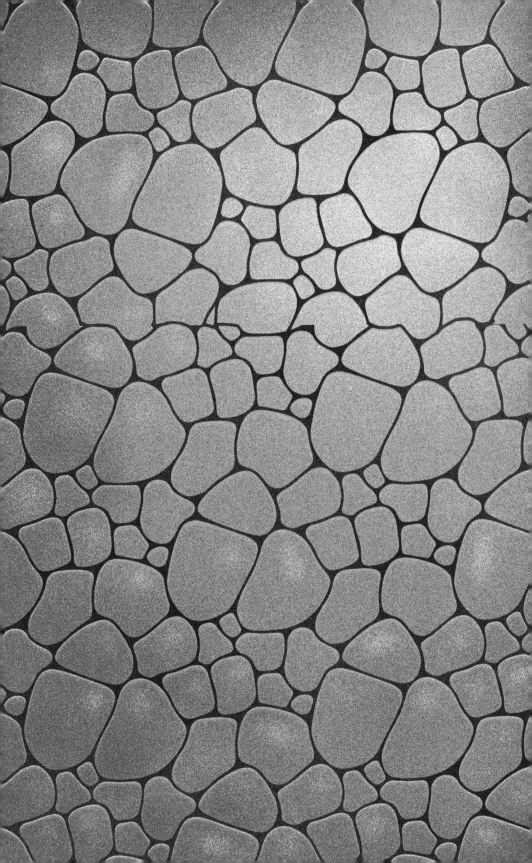

The War of the Titans

In the earliest times, the universe was ruled by Uranus, the sky in human form. His wife was **Gaea**, the earth, and their children were the **Titans**—mighty beings who possessed the strength of the earthquake, hurricane, and volcano.

A crafty Titan named **Cronus** desired Uranus's throne. One night he snuck through the darkness and wounded his father with a single slice of his scythe. Stripped of his power, Uranus retreated into the heavens and remained there, a dethroned king.

As Cronus claimed his father's place as lord of the universe, he heard the voice of his mother, Gaea, whispering in his ear. "Be careful, son. Just as you have dethroned your father, one of your children will do the same to you."

Cronus brushed this warning aside, sat upon Uranus's throne, and made the Titan **Rhea** his queen. Yet as they began their own royal family, the prophecy echoed in his mind—one of his children would overthrow him. Cronus vowed that none would ever have the chance.

Soon Rhea gave birth to a child, a perfect baby girl named **Hestia**, the first of the **gods**, the next generation of beings after the Titans. Instead of cradling the newborn in his arms, Cronus snatched her up and swallowed her. Rhea was horrified, but Cronus shook his scythe at her. "No child of mine shall ever betray me!"

Four more divine children followed—**Demeter**, **Hera**, **Hades**, and **Poseidon**—and they, too, were gobbled up by their father. Finally, Rhea could bear it no more. She resolved that her next child would not suffer the same fate.

When the time came for her next baby to be born, Rhea flew away to a secret cave on the island of **Crete**. There she gave birth to a strong baby boy named **Zeus**. She put him into the care

of Gaea, saying,
"Mother, protect
my son until he is
strong enough to
challenge Cronus."

Rhea returned to
her husband—but
not without a plan.
With his belly bulg-
ing over the side of
his throne, Cronus

bellowed, "Where is the newest child?" Rhea held
out a bundle wrapped tightly in cloth. Cronus
grabbed it and gulped it down. He had no idea that
he was not swallowing a baby at all, but a rock in
disguise. Rhea smiled to herself.

Years passed. Safely hidden on Crete, Zeus grew
from a baby into a fully-grown god. When Gaea saw
the time was right, she whispered to him of his tyran-
nical father and how Zeus could overthrow him. He
traveled to his father's palace. With Rhea's help, Zeus
slipped a secret concoction into Cronus's royal cup.

Upon taking a drink, Cronus sensed something
was wrong. "What is happening?" he cried, grasping
his throat. Then he began to purge the contents of his

stomach. Up came his swallowed children—Hestia, Demeter, Hera, Hades, and Poseidon, all bursting forth with a glorious light. In his belly, they had not died, but grown to adulthood.

Finally, up came the rock he had swallowed in the place of Zeus. Cronus gaped at the rock and then at his wife in shock. Zeus stood by her side. "Looking for me, Father?"

Cronus bellowed with rage, and his scythe flashed with fire—summoning all his Titan brothers and sisters to rally to his call. Zeus yelled for his siblings to arm themselves and prepare for the battle to end all battles. Quick as a flash, Zeus flew to the **Underworld** to free the children of Gaea whom Uranus had trapped there long ago. Among the freed creatures were three **Cyclopes**, one-eyed giants, who quickly forged three mighty weapons for the gods—a **trident** for Poseidon, a helmet of invisibility for Hades, and thunderbolts for Zeus. Now armed, the gods faced off against the Titans.

The Titans fought with all the forces of nature. They summoned winds to fling the gods against the mountains. They called blasts of fire down from the sky and ripped up chunks of the earth to hurl at the gods. The gods fought just as fiercely.

As Hera, Hestia, and Demeter used their powers to deflect these blows, Poseidon raised his trident to summon ocean waves to crash against the Titans and Hades used his helmet of invisibility to attack them from behind. Then Zeus entered the battle. Flying down from the heavens, he unleashed his thunderbolts—blasts of power that rocketed through the sky and battered the Titans. From one end of the earth to the other, their conflict shook the mountains to their foundations and caused the seas to boil. In the end, the gods were victorious.

Realizing all was lost, Cronus fled to the far regions of the earth, never to return. The rest of the Titans weren't so fortunate. Zeus punished them for warring against the gods. One towering Titan named Atlas was forced to hold up the sky. The rest were chained in the darkest region of the Underworld.

Zeus made himself a palace on top of **Mount Olympus**, the highest mountain in Greece. From there he would rule the universe. Gaea's prophecy had come true: The Titan who had overthrown his father had suffered the same fate at the hands of his own child.

Prometheus, the Fire Thief

The destructive war between the gods and the Titans had ended, and the earth lay scorched and barren. Zeus, the leader of the gods, punished all the Titans, except for two. A wise Titan named Prometheus and his brother, Epimetheus, had not fought alongside the others, so Zeus released them into the world. "Go in freedom," Zeus said. "But remember—I will be watching."

Prometheus and Epimetheus walked the wounded earth, and together they worked at restoring its beauty. As they did so, Prometheus was troubled. "Even if we rebuild the world, it will still be empty," he said. "It needs new life."

At a riverside, he took a bit of clay into his hands. Using his skillful fingers, he shaped it into the form of an animal. "Look, Epimetheus!" said Prometheus. "I have made a new creature. Why don't you use your power to give it a special gift?" Epimetheus did, and the newly created rabbit hopped away with a swift pair of legs. Then Prometheus repeated the process, time and time again. Prometheus presented each new creature to Epimetheus, who gave it a unique ability—far-seeing eyes, spiny quills, a long tail, or a sticky tongue.

Although Prometheus created countless creatures, they all lacked something special. "Hmmm," he said. "None of these creatures has a divine quality. They all look downward at the earth. I want to make a creature that will look to the sky . . . and dream." So in the clay beside a river, he fashioned a new creature—one in the form of a god. He called it man.

"Now give man a gift like all the other creatures," said Prometheus to his brother.

Epimetheus moved to do so, then stopped. "Oh no! I have given them all away. There are no more special gifts to give." Epimetheus was never thinking ahead.

Prometheus shrugged. "It is no problem. Man will not need the abilities given to the animals. I will give him the most powerful gift of all: a cunning mind."

Prometheus formed man after man from the clay, breathing life into them one by one. With the pride of a parent, he watched as they stumbled like newborns about the earth, learning how to see and taste and touch.

Soon cold winds began to blow, and Prometheus's creations shuddered and huddled together for warmth. Then the unthinkable happened: One of the men grew still and died. "No!" cried Prometheus. He felt the cold body. "My creatures have nothing to keep them warm—nothing to protect them from the wild animals of the forest." Prometheus knew there was one thing that could keep man safe: fire. But only the gods possessed fire.

The Titan looked heavenward to where fire glowed in the forge of Mount Olympus. "Zeus already distrusts us," said Prometheus. "The gods will never give fire to man willingly." He knew what he must do. He set his jaw, plucked a hollow reed, and snuck up to Mount Olympus. He caught a bit of the gods' forge fire inside the hollow reed and returned the gift to earth, distributing it among his sons.

When Zeus looked down and saw that fire now dotted the dark landscape, his rage was fierce. "I knew better than to trust a Titan!" He ordered his servants to arrest Prometheus at once, and they dragged the Titan before Zeus's throne.

Prometheus denied nothing. "I stole fire to save my creations," he said. "And I would do it again."

Zeus stared at him with hatred. "Bind this traitor to a mountain peak with unbreakable chains!" There he would be eternally punished. Each day Zeus's eagle, his special servant, would come and tear at Prometheus's body. Each evening Prometheus would heal, only to be torn again the next day and the next for all eternity.

But Zeus did not stop there. Prometheus's new human creations must also be punished for daring to claim fire as their own. Zeus filled a jar with all the evils imaginable—every type of sorrow and misfortune—and sent it to Epimetheus. Along with the jar he also sent a creation fashioned by the gods: Pandora, the first woman.

Failing to think ahead once again, Epimetheus foolishly accepted this present from Zeus without suspicion. He took both Pandora and her jar into his home. Written on the jar was a message not to open it under any circumstances, but Pandora's curiosity got the better of her. She had to know what was inside. When she lifted the lid off the jar, all the evil came shrieking out, filling the world with all sorts of trouble. Life would forever be a struggle because of this trick of Zeus.

As Epimetheus and Pandora stared at the seemingly empty jar, something stirred inside it. The last thing to exit the jar was a feathery wisp of hope. For all the misfortune Zeus had unleashed on human beings, this bit of hope would make life bearable.

Demeter and Persephone

 lthough Zeus's palace on Mount Olympus made an excellent home for the gods, Demeter, the goddess of the harvest, decided to live on the earth. "I must be down where things are green and growing," she said, smiling. Together with her daughter, the goddess Persephone, Demeter tended the greenery of the earth, making it grow and blossom. But Persephone caught the eye of Hades, the Lord of the Underworld, watching from his dark kingdom. He knew Demeter would never let her daughter marry him willingly, so he devised a plan.

As Persephone gathered flowers alone one day in a secluded meadow, the ground beneath her quaked. The earth split open, and the chariot of Hades roared up from the inky blackness.

Persephone cried for help, but the god whisked her onto his chariot and disappeared below the earth—sealing the ground shut above him.

It did not take long for Demeter to discover that Persephone was missing. "Help! Help!" she cried. "Someone has stolen my daughter—my life and my joy!" But no one heeded her cry. No one offered her assistance or even comfort.

Heartbroken and alone, Demeter wandered the earth with weary steps, searching for any sign of Persephone. "Please! Have you seen my daughter?" she asked in each place she traveled. No one could give her any news of Persephone.

As Demeter's despair deepened, all warmth vanished from the air, and all richness left the soil.

Blossoms wilted, trees lost their leaves, and crops withered. The earth was becoming as cold and lifeless as Demeter's heart. The gods saw that something must be done, and they called out to Demeter to remember her duty to the earth and its people.

"What has the earth done for me?" Demeter sobbed. "It has taken my daughter and hidden her from me. Let it die!"

Finally, **Helios**, the god of the sun, heard of Demeter's anguish. He alone knew the truth about Persephone. He called down from the heavens, "I saw Hades take your daughter and carry her into the Underworld. Seek your daughter there!"

This news stunned Demeter, and she cried out to Zeus for justice. "If you do not return my daughter to me, the entire world will die!"

So Zeus sent **Hermes**, the clever messenger of the gods, to command Hades to release Persephone before the world wasted away completely.

Hermes used his winged sandals to fly into the depths of the earth to the Underworld, where the souls of the dead reside and Hades rules over them in silent power. Hermes found Hades and his captive bride seated side-by-side on twin thrones.

Persephone's youthful radiance was now muted by the shadows of the Underworld. But when Hermes issued Zeus's command to release Persephone, a bit of life seemed to return to her eyes.

Hades only scowled. "What right does my little brother have to order me around?"

Hermes held up his winged staff, the symbol of the power given to him by Zeus. "Careful. It's best not to anger Zeus."

Hades knew he had no choice. "Very well," he said in defeat. "She may go."

As Hermes flew back earthward, Hades turned to Persephone with a look of sadness. "I am sorry for what I have done, my dear. I stole you away from your mother, and I have no right to keep you here against your will. But before you go, take this parting gift." He held up a pomegranate fruit.

"Thank you for this gift," said Persephone, taking it up and tasting some of its seeds. "Farewell!"

Persephone rose from the darkness of the Underworld back to the light of the world. The reunion of Demeter and Persephone was a sight to behold. All of creation felt its power, for the earth was once again bathed in the glow of their love.

"My daughter! You are back for good," said Demeter through tears. "But wait! Please tell me you did not eat any of the food of the Underworld."

Persephone's smile faded. "Yes, but only four tiny seeds."

Demeter wilted. "Anyone who tastes the food of the Underworld must remain there."

It seemed all was lost, but Hermes urged them not to despair. "Only four seeds? I'm sure Zeus can strike a deal."

He carried this news to Zeus, who was able to make a compromise with his grim brother. Persephone would not remain in the Underworld permanently. Each year, she would rejoin her husband in the Underworld for four months, one for each seed. After these months had passed, she would return in all her glory.

For this reason there are warm months where Demeter is joyous—basking in the presence of her daughter—followed by cold months when her heart breaks anew. The earth grows cold, and crops will not grow until the return of Persephone, the goddess of springtime.

Apollo versus Python

The Titan **Leto** fled through the wilderness. She was about to give birth to twin gods, but she was on the run and had nowhere to go. Her powerful enemy, Hera, queen of the gods, had cursed her by declaring, "No land will give Leto shelter, or it will face my wrath!" She also summoned a terrible, scaly monster from the earth—the dreaded Python—to pursue Leto as she fled.

Hera's anger was legendary, so every patch of land where Leto tried to rest drove her away. In vain she begged, "Please! I just need a place to give birth to my children!" At last Poseidon, the god of the seas, took pity on her. He raised

an island called **Delos** from the sea. It was just a bobbing piece of earth, not connected to the mainland and not subject to Hera's commandment. The sea god whisked Leto away to the floating island. Python could not reach her there, so he slunk away into his deep cave.

Safe on the island of Delos, Leto gave birth to her twins: two of the greatest gods of Olympus. Leto's first child was a goddess as luminous as the moon. She would one day grow up to be the huntress **Artemis**. Her second child was a shining god, **Apollo**—destined to be the god of light, truth, and music.

Soon after this, Zeus descended to Delos to visit the newborn gods. He presented each child with a bow and a quiver full of arrows. The arrows of Artemis shone with moonglow, and the arrows of Apollo were like shafts of light. Then Zeus blessed the island of Delos for giving Leto safety and asked Poseidon to secure it to the bottom of the sea.

As Apollo grew from a baby into a young man, he was determined to prove himself as one of the finest gods. He went to Leto to ask her advice. "Mother, since I am young among the gods, I must perform some great deed to prove my worth. Is there an evil in the world that I can conquer?"

"Oh, my son," said Leto. "I know of an evil greater than any other—a monster called Python. He has all the strength of a god and feeds on beasts and humans alike. He even pursued me once. Fortunately, I escaped. Be careful, though. Python breathes poisonous fumes and fights with all the strength of the earth."

"I have heard enough!" Apollo declared, rising with his bow in hand. "Where can I find this monster?"

"Python lives near **Delphi**," she replied. "His lair is a cave in the side of **Mount Parnassus**—a cave so deep, some say it is the center of the earth."

Bidding his mother farewell, Apollo flew to Mount Parnassus and approached Python's cave—his bow and arrows of light at the ready. When his feet touched down upon the mountain-side, it sent a shudder deep into the ground. "Come forth, earth-dragon!" Apollo thundered. "The god of light is here to destroy you once and for all."

The entire mountain shook, and a deafening roar came out of the mouth of the cave. Many would have fled right then, but Apollo boldly stood his ground. Then Python appeared. He slithered out of the cave, his long body crowned by a broad, flat head, deadly fangs, and fiery eyes. Python extended himself high into the air, so high that he seemed to blot out the sun. "You dare challenge me, puny god?" he asked with a hissing laugh.

"I do," said Apollo, blazing brilliantly. "And I will be victorious."

"How can you be so sure?"

"I am the god of truth, and I cannot lie."

"Hmmm," said Python. "You cannot lie, but can you die?"

With lightning-quick speed, Python struck at Apollo, but the god dodged the attack. Drawing his divine bow, Apollo released his arrows, which blazed through the air. Clouds of poisonous fumes billowed from Python's mouth, and fire flew from his nostrils. The light god and the monster fought for hours—up and down the mountain. Finally, one of Apollo's arrows hit home, piercing Python's thick skin. The monster shuddered and died.

Apollo dragged Python's body into its deep lair and hurled it down into a chasm. Brushing off his hands, the god looked around at the cavern. "To honor my victory, I shall make my **temple** here," he said.

Apollo appointed a **priestess** called Pythia, named as a reminder of Python's defeat. He made her a golden, three-legged stool, which she placed near the cleft in the earth that held Python's body. "You shall be my messenger," he told her. "People will come from all over Greece to hear your wise words." And it was true. The **oracle** of Delphi became a source of wisdom

throughout the world. Generals came to ask her to predict the outcomes of their battles, and adventurers came to hear their fortunes. In the former home of Python, she received the words of Apollo, the god of light and truth.

Artemis, the Goddess of the Hunt

rtemis was the goddess of the hunt, and she was never happier than when she was running barefoot through the wild woods. She loved the feel of pine needles beneath her feet, the wind in her face, and her bow in her hand. Although she was the hunter-in-chief of the gods, she loved all the animals of the woodland and was their special protector against cruel treatment.

But sometimes the hunter becomes the hunted. Once, a pair of giants became so enamored with Artemis's luminous beauty that they tried to capture her. Outrunning them was no trouble for the nimble goddess, but they

pursued her relentlessly—all throughout the world. Finally, they chased her into a grove of trees by the sea. As they entered the grove, all they saw there was a single deer, watching them with shining eyes.

"Where did the goddess go?" one giant asked.

"She's right there!" the other responded. "She thinks she can fool us by changing forms. Let's teach her a lesson!"

The giants crept to either side of their prey, then rose and hurled their spears with all their might. This was their last mistake. The foolish giants did not realize that while they were aiming at the deer, they were also aiming at each other. The deer leapt high over the spears, which found their marks—ending the giants' lives.

Settling gently back down to the ground, the deer transformed into the glowing form of Artemis. "That will teach you to hunt *me*," she said with a smile. "I can't wait to tell Apollo about this."

Artemis's twin brother was Apollo, the god of light. No brother and sister were more devoted. Even though Artemis's most common hunting companions were a band of woodland **nymphs**, Apollo was allowed to join them. Artemis's rule was: No boys allowed—except for Apollo.

That is, until she met Orion.

One day while running through the forests of Crete, Artemis drew up short. Before her stood a young man with a lion's pelt thrown over his shoulder and a club in his hand. "Be careful, mortal," she said. "Have you come to challenge me? I am Artemis!"

The young man smiled. "Of course not! I have heard stories of what happens to those who challenge *you*. I am Orion, and I would love to hunt with you—if you will let me."

Artemis smiled at his boldness. "Try to keep up—if you can."

Orion surprised Artemis. He was mortal, but his skill at hunting was almost like a god's. Soon Artemis and Orion spent all their time together. This left no time for Apollo, who grew jealous.

Apollo spied on his sister and Orion as they hunted, searching for some way to ruin their friendship. One day he heard Orion make a foolish boast: He claimed that he was such a good hunter, he would eventually slay every beast on earth. Apollo chuckled. "Now I will get rid of Orion once and for all."

Apollo flew to Gaea, the earth, and told her of Orion's boast. Gaea was dismayed. She called forth a new creature—one designed to kill. The dust of the earth swirled to life and took on the form of a scorpion with a venomous stinger tail. Gaea sent it to attack Orion.

Orion was all alone when the scorpion came bursting through the trees—striking at him with its deadly pinchers and barbed tail. Orion feebly blocked its strikes with his club. His skills were no match for the scorpion. Perhaps if Artemis had been with him, things would have been different. The scorpion drove him to the edge of the sea, and he dove in to save himself. The scorpion hissed as Orion swam away.

Watching from afar, Apollo growled, "No! He's escaping."

Apollo found Artemis hunting nearby. "Care for an archery wager, sister?" he asked. "Or do you no longer have time for your brother?"

"Only if you care to lose," said Artemis.

"Let's see. Now for a target," said Apollo, turning slyly toward the sea. "See that little black speck moving across the waves? I bet you cannot hit it."

"I bet I can," said Artemis, unslinging her silver bow and nocking an arrow. She took aim—not knowing she was about to end the life of her friend—and let the shaft fly. *Shunk!* The black speck sank out of sight. "There," she said, lowering her bow. "You have lost the wager."

"But I've won something even better," said Apollo.

"What do you mean?" asked Artemis.

Because he could speak no false words, Apollo admitted to his sister what he had done.

Artemis's face flashed with anger. "How could you? Your immature jealousy has cost me my friend!"

Artemis ran to the beach, where she found the body of Orion washed ashore. "You will never be forgotten," she whispered, raising Orion's figure into the stars. To this day he still shines down from the heavens in the form of a constellation. As a reminder of his fate, Artemis placed the scorpion there, too—still pursuing Orion with its deadly stinger.

A City for Athena

Zeus had a horrible headache. He groaned upon his throne, powerless against the pressure and pain. "Something must be done about this splitting headache!" he cried. "Wait! Splitting! That's it!"

Zeus called for an axe and commanded the other gods to strike him with it in the head. Because Zeus was a god, it did not kill him. Instead, it opened his skull and allowed what was inside to come out.

As the other gods stared in amazement, a grown woman sprang from Zeus's head, wearing golden armor and carrying a mighty spear. She was **Athena**, the goddess of wisdom.

"No wonder I had a headache!" said Zeus in awe. "I had a new daughter growing in there."

Athena soon proved to be one of the wisest and most powerful gods. She invented the arts of cooking and sewing for mortals and designed the first ship that could sail in either direction without turning. When an army of angry giants tried to scale Mount Olympus, Athena hoisted an entire island out of the sea and used it to crush them.

As she grew in renown, Athena realized she did not have a patron city. These were cities that worshipped a certain god most of all. In return, their patron god paid special attention to the city's well-being. Athena wanted a city like that.

In the region of **Attica** there was an unnamed city that did not yet have a patron god. It was built on a hill called Acropolis with plains around it, and its king was a strange creature named Cecrops, who had the top half of a man and the bottom half of a snake.

"Hmmm," said Athena to herself. "It is said that King Cecrops had no father and mother but was born out of the earth. My birth is unusual as well. Maybe this is the city for me."

Athena descended from Mount Olympus to speak to Cecrops and offer to be the city's protector. As Athena appeared to Cecrops, so did Poseidon, god of the sea.

"What are you doing here, Athena?" growled Poseidon, brandishing his trident. "I've come to claim this city for myself!"

"Well, uncle," replied Athena calmly, "so have I."

At first Cecrops was startled by two gods appearing out of thin air before him, but then he leaned back in his throne. "Interesting! Two of the most powerful gods want to protect my city? What do you have to offer?"

"Choose me, King," said Poseidon. "I have always been a friend of mortals. It was I who created the most magnificent creature ever made: the horse. I summoned it from the surging waves of the sea!"

"Yes, that was an impressive creation," said Athena, "until the humans realized they could not tame it. Not until *I* invented a bridle, the headgear used to control the horse!"

Athena turned to Cecrops. "King, I say we have a contest. Whoever gives this city the most useful gift shall be its protector."

"A fine idea!" said Cecrops.

"Very well," growled Poseidon, "but *I* will go first."

"May the best god win," said Athena confidently.

Poseidon went to the Acropolis. "Behold! I will provide water for the city." At these words, a spring bubbled up from the ground, and the mortals murmured in amazement.

But Athena saw the flaw in this gift. "Still thinking like a sea god, are you? What good will a *salty* spring do for these people? Humans only drink fresh water."

Poseidon raged, "Let's see you do any better!"

"Watch and learn," said Athena. She raised her powerful arms, and a tree grew from the ground. "Behold! The first olive tree! The people can harvest its fruit to eat. The oil from the olives can light their lamps and cook their food. They can build their boats and houses from its wood."

The mortals applauded Athena's gift. It was obviously the more useful of the two.

Cecrops issued his verdict: "I must say that Athena's gift is superior. She shall be the protector of our city." The people cheered.

Poseidon would not be beaten so easily. "Name this worthless city whatever you want! It will soon be underwater!" He raised his trident, struck the earth, and disappeared with a snarl. In the distance, the sea began to rise, flooding the plains below.

Cecrops turned to Athena. "We chose you as our protector! Now protect us!"

"Do not fear," she said. "This is just the blustering of a sore loser." Then she called out in her mighty voice. "Hear me, citizens! Come to the Acropolis! I will not let the flood waters reach you here." As the waters continued to rise, the people of the plains hurried to the Acropolis.

Although Poseidon's waters swelled and raged, they could never reach the high hill. Finally, they receded, and the city was preserved.

Cecrops named the city Athens in honor of Athena, and she made it a center of learning and knowledge for the people of Greece. In eternal gratitude, the citizens built a massive temple, the Parthenon, dedicated to the goddess of wisdom.

Hephaestus, the God of Fire

p on Mount Olympus, Zeus and his wife, Hera, were having an argument. Hera was irked because Zeus had created a new daughter, Athena, all by himself out of his head. He had not stopped bragging about it since.

"He is so smug!" Hera said. "Does he think he's the only one who can have a miracle child?" Hera decided she would make a child all by herself, too. She closed her eyes and concentrated as hard as she could, and when she opened them again, a little god, a son, was sitting upon her lap. "Look! I've done it!" she cried.

Hera named her new son **Hephaestus** and proclaimed his birth a victory. But the other gods were not so sure. Hera's little boy did not look like the other gods. He was short and stout with a bright shock of red hair that stuck up like flame. He had also been born with a twisted foot and walked with a limp.

Zeus was especially annoyed by Hephaestus. The fire-haired god was clumsy and lumbering, and he did not seem to have any special talents. Plus, Hera was always using Hephaestus's birth as proof that she was just as powerful as he was.

Things came to a head one day when Zeus and Hera were having yet another argument, and the peace-loving Hephaestus stepped in to defend his mother. Zeus was consumed by rage. Seizing Hephaestus by the leg, Zeus flung him off Mount Olympus. Hephaestus fell for a whole day—blazing like a comet—until he landed on the island of **Lemnos** and rolled into the sea.

A kind sea nymph named **Thetis** lifted Hephaestus from the waves. "The poor little thing," she said, cradling him tenderly in her arms. "He will come and live with me." So Thetis raised Hephaestus in her seaside cave.

As Hephaestus grew, he often asked his foster mother about his birth. "I did not have a father—only a mother. Does that make me strange?"

"Many gods are born in unique ways," Thetis replied. "Why, **Aphrodite**, the most beautiful goddess of all, was born out of the sea foam! Now she is the goddess of love and beauty."

"But what am I the god of?" asked Hephaestus. "The god of clumsiness? The god of limping?"

"Those things do not matter. Every god has a special skill—something only they can do," said Thetis. "You must discover what yours is and rejoin the other gods on Mount Olympus."

Hephaestus frowned. "They cast me out! Why would I return there?"

"To teach them to look deeper," said Thetis.

Hephaestus took Thetis's advice to heart. He was a wise god, and he possessed the ability to shape metal and craft new things. He hollowed out a mountain on Lemnos, built a forge inside, and began crafting the greatest treasures imaginable. To assist him in his work, he designed three gold-plated maidens with insides filled with gears. When he was at work in his forge, fire would come out of the top of the mountain like a chimney.

Thetis watched her foster son's work with pride. Years passed, and Hephaestus was now a fully-grown god with a bushy, red beard to match his wild head of hair.

One day he said, "I am ready to return." Thetis bid him a fond farewell.

When Hephaestus arrived on Mount Olympus, he made quite an entrance. He walked into the palace followed by his mechanical maidens, their arms full of treasures like the gods had never seen.

"What is the meaning of this?" asked Zeus gruffly.

Hephaestus bowed humbly. "You cast me off Olympus, mighty Zeus," he said. "You thought I was useless and clumsy. But I have returned to show you my skill. I may be different, but I can do things none of the rest of you can."

The gods watched in stunned silence as Hephaestus displayed his treasures one by one—an engraved shield for Zeus, a throne for Hera, a golden bow for Apollo. Hephaestus had crafted each of the gods a special gift.

"But we were not kind to you," said the gods. "We treated you poorly."

"That does not mean I cannot be kind to *you*," said Hephaestus with a smile.

The gods looked at one another sheepishly, but Zeus was the most ashamed of all. "Please stay with us here on Olympus. We have mistreated you, and for that, we are truly sorry."

"I accept, because I see you have learned your lesson," said Hephaestus. "Sometimes you must look deeper to see someone's true worth."

"Well said!" Zeus replied, clapping the squat fire god upon the back. "From this day forward, I declare Hephaestus shall be the god of the fire and the forge!"

Eros and Psyche

Aphrodite was the goddess of love, yet sometimes her behavior was less than lovely. When she heard about the god-like beauty of a mortal princess named Psyche, she summoned her son, **Eros**. Eros was a handsome winged god whose weapon was a bow with two types of arrows. One caused love and the other hardheartedness. Burning with jealousy, Aphrodite commanded him to curse the princess by causing her to fall in love with the nastiest man alive.

Eros was used to doing his mother's dirty work, but when he found Psyche, he was instantly charmed by her. Everything she did was full of kindness and grace. For the first time, Eros felt the love he caused in others.

43

"Oh, if only I could ask Psyche to be *my* wife,"
Eros said to himself. "But my mother would never
allow me to marry a mortal—especially one she
despises. But wait! Perhaps if it were a secret!" He
winged himself away with a plan for how he and
Psyche could be together.

The next day, Psyche's family received terrible
news. An oracle declared that Psyche must be left
on a nearby mountaintop, where a monster would
come to take her away for its bride. Her family had
no choice but to comply, but before they left her,
they pressed a dagger into her hand. "We cannot
save you," they said. "But you can save yourself."

Psyche waited bravely. Suddenly, she felt the
wind lifting her into the air. The wind carried her
to a golden palace high in the mountains. Invisible
servants guided her into the magnificent halls.
"Where is my husband?" she asked.

"He will be here at nightfall," they replied.

When night fell, Psyche waited in the palace, her
dagger hidden under her cloak. Then a voice spoke
out of the darkness. To her surprise, the voice was
kind. "Psyche, I am your husband. Each night I will
visit you, but by morning I will be gone. You must

never see me. If you do, you will have to leave this place forever."

A strange routine began. Psyche spent each night with her husband, but never saw him. As days turned into weeks, Psyche realized something even more strange: Monster or not, she loved her husband. Yet doubt crept in. Why all this secrecy?

Psyche decided she must know the truth. The next night, after her husband had fallen asleep, she drew her dagger and lit an oil lamp—casting its light upon him. Instead of a monster, she saw a handsome young man, his white wings folded in sleep. She moved to snuff the lamp, but as she did, a drop of its oil fell upon his shoulder. His eyes flew open, and he saw the drawn dagger. Psyche tried to explain, but Eros cried out, "Why have you done this? I thought I could keep you safe from my mother if I kept my identity a secret. I am Eros, the god of love. But love cannot live where there is no trust!" There was a rush of wind, their palace home vanished, and Psyche was alone.

It seemed that all was lost, but Psyche did not give up. "Eros risked his mother's anger to be with me," she said. "I must do the same." So she called to Aphrodite and begged her to let her see Eros once again.

"Fine," Aphrodite sneered, appearing before the girl. "If you complete a series of tasks of *my* choosing!"

Aphrodite had no intention of being fair. She sent Psyche on a series of impossible errands. Each time the strength of Psyche's spirit allowed her to succeed. For the final task, Aphrodite sent Psyche into the land of the dead. "Go to Persephone, the Queen of the Underworld, and ask her to put a bit of her beauty in this box."

Psyche journeyed into the dark Underworld and came face-to-face with Queen Persephone. There she unfolded her sad tale. "Mortal princess," Persephone replied. "I can see your love is true, and for that I will give you a bit of my beauty."

Overjoyed, Psyche returned earthward with the box of beauty in hand. Then doubt struck again. The box felt so empty. She needed to take a peek to see if the beauty was really there. When she inched open the lid, the beauty billowed out and disappeared. Defeated, Psyche fell to the ground senseless.

When she awoke, Eros's smiling face was looking into hers. "You really do love me, Psyche!"

"But we can never be together," she said sadly.

"Perhaps there is a way." Eros carried Psyche all the way to Mount Olympus, and there, they presented their case to Zeus, who was moved by Eros's love and Psyche's strong spirit. But their pleas were interrupted as Aphrodite appeared. "No!" she cried. "A god cannot marry a mortal!"

"You are absolutely right," said Zeus. "That is why I must make Psyche a goddess!" Zeus did just that. So Eros, the greatest of hearts, and Psyche, the strongest of spirits, were joined together forever.

Echo and Narcissus

Love is wonderful when it is shared, but what happens when it is only one-sided? Echo was a nymph, a nature spirit of the woodlands. She was also an eager talker who loved to bend the ear of anyone who would listen. One day, Hera, the queen of the gods, appeared in the forest where Echo lived, searching for her husband. "Where is Zeus?" she asked quickly when she spotted Echo. "He's always leaving Mount Olympus and lying about where he's going! This time I want to catch him red-handed!"

Undaunted by Hera's fury, Echo began to chatter away. "Oh, Queen Hera! I am so pleased to meet you! You are looking for your husband, you say? The noble Zeus? Well, my, my! What a parade of royal visitors we are having today. Just yesterday, I was telling the other nymphs ... "

Suddenly, Hera saw Zeus appear over the distant treetops, flying back to Mount Olympus. "Argh!" cried Hera. "He got away ... while I was busy listening to you!" She turned on the nymph, her eyes filling with fury. "Because you are so fond of talking, I will curse you in the worst possible way!" There was a flash of light, and Hera was gone.

Echo's sister nymphs ran out to find out what had happened, but when Echo opened her mouth to tell them, no words came out.

"What is the matter?" they asked. "Have you lost your voice?"

"Your voice," Echo blurted helplessly. "Your voice."

What was happening? In tears, Echo fled from the other nymphs.

"Echo!" they cried. "Where are you going?"

Echo covered her mouth to keep the words inside, but she could not hold them back.

"Going," she said. "Going."

Hera had cursed Echo so that she could no longer speak her own words—only repeat the last words spoken to her. Echo hid in the deepest part of the forest. She had lost all hope for the future.

One day she saw a young man walking through the woods—the most handsome young man she had ever seen. At the sight of him, hope stirred within her once again.

"Even though I am cursed, perhaps this beautiful man could love me," Echo thought to herself.

What Echo did not know is that this man was **Narcissus**. While many women had longed for him to love them, he was cruel and vain and had broken their hearts. As Echo followed him, the man heard her rustling in the underbrush.

"Is someone here?" asked Narcissus. Echo saw her chance and stepped out of the underbrush.

"Here!" she cried. "Here!"

Narcissus wrinkled his handsome nose. "Have you come to stare at me like all the others? Why would *you* be worthy of my love?"

"Love?" Echo repeated sadly. "Love?"

"I would die before I gave someone like you power over me," he sneered.

"Over me," Echo said, disappearing back into the forest. "Over me."

Narcissus turned away with a smirk and continued his journey. In his mind no one was good enough for him. In fact, there had been a **prophecy** when he was born: "Narcissus shall have a long life . . . only if he never discovers himself."

Nemesis, the goddess of righteous anger, had witnessed Narcissus's treatment of Echo and many others, and she decided to punish him for his arrogance. "If he will not love others, I will doom him to fall in love with only himself!"

Leaving Echo's forest behind, Narcissus traveled high into the mountains, where crystal clear springs gush forth from the rocky ground. He was thirsty, so he bent over a mirror-like pool to drink.

As he did, his heart stopped. Before him, in the pool of water, he saw a face as beautiful as his own.

"Who is this I see before me?" he gasped. "Now I know the love that others have spoken of!" Nemesis had clouded Narcissus's mind, so he did not know that he gazed upon his own reflection. Time and time again, he tried to grasp his love trapped within the pool, but when he did, the image faded. "Don't go, my sweet! Don't go! I see I must leave you in your watery prison, but never will I leave you! I will sit here by this pool—day and night—until you come forth and I can claim you as my love."

That is what he did. At last, from days without food, Narcissus drew his final breath. "Farewell."

Echo watched from a distance, sadly repeating his final words. "Farewell. Farewell."

Miserable and alone, Echo hid in a mountain cave. She became one with the darkness. All that was left of her was her voice. To this day, when people journey where earth and stone rule, they can still hear Echo repeating their words back to them.

Meanwhile, on the spot where Narcissus had died, a flower had bloomed. It was the narcissus flower, whose head droops down over the water, hoping to catch a glimpse of its own reflection.

Orpheus and Eurydice

ike love, music is one of life's most powerful forces. It gives us strength when we are weak and comforts us when we are sad. But is music mightier than death?

It was no surprise that **Orpheus** was the most talented musician who had ever lived. After all, Orpheus's father was Apollo, the god of music himself, and his mother was **Calliope**, one of the nine eternal muses, goddesses who inspired every type of art. When Orpheus was just a boy, Apollo descended from Mount Olympus to present his son with a golden **lyre**, which he taught him to play with the skill of a god. Likewise, Calliope taught Orpheus how to compose

songs and sing them with his beautiful voice. These lessons worked so well that Orpheus's music had supernatural powers. His mystical notes could charm wild animals, move rocks and trees, and change the course of rivers. In lesser hands such power could have been used for selfish gain, but Orpheus was a true artist—a pure-hearted lover of beauty.

It did not take long for love to find Orpheus. As he wandered through the wide world, he met a young woman named **Eurydice** who charmed his heart, and they were married at once. But their happiness did not last long. Soon after their wedding, while Eurydice wandered in a meadow, a venomous snake bit her, and she died.

Before this time, Orpheus's music had been filled with light and hope. After Eurydice's death, Orpheus only played songs of mourning. His songs still held power, but instead of bringing sunshine and warmth, they caused clouds to cover the sky and cold rain to fall. As Orpheus wandered the countryside, weeping and playing his sad laments, even the gods pitied him and suggested that Orpheus seek his lost love in the Underworld. Perhaps his music was powerful enough to do the impossible. Perhaps it could bring back the dead.

For the first time in many months, Orpheus felt hope. "Maybe the gods are right," he said. "I will use my songs to win Eurydice back from death."

Orpheus turned his steps toward the dark Underworld, where even the bravest adventurers fear to go. He was armed only with his music, but this was the only weapon he needed. As Orpheus approached **Cerberus**, the three-headed guard dog of Hades, he strummed and sang more loudly. Mesmerized by Orpheus's notes, the snarling beast ceased its barking and slunk to the side of the path. Soon the musician neared the river **Styx**, a river no mortal can pass without first paying a coin. The ferryman, **Charon**,

who ferries souls across, held out his bony hand for the toll. Orpheus had no coin, but he continued singing. Charon's hand closed, and he allowed

Orpheus into his boat and ferried him across the river—without payment.

Finally, Orpheus reached the palace of Hades, where the Lord of the Underworld sat emotionlessly upon his throne. Orpheus sang with all his skill, "All souls must come to this dark and silent world. Death is a debt that must always be paid. But I search for one who came to you too soon. A flower plucked before it had a chance to bloom."

Then the impossible happened: The stone-cold heart of Hades broke, and tears of iron ran down his cheek. "You may take the soul of the one you love from my realm . . . under one condition," he said. "Her soul will follow you back to the living world above, but you must never look back at her until she is in the earth's light once again, or to me she must return. Light to light. Shadow to shadow."

Orpheus happily agreed to these terms and began his journey back toward the surface. But as he walked, he could hear no footsteps behind him. He began to wonder, "Did Hades trick me?" Just one peek over his shoulder would tell him that Eurydice was truly following him. "No," he said to himself. "I must trust that she is there."

In the distance ahead Orpheus could see the light of the world once again, and he raced toward it. Eurydice would be alive once again! As soon as his foot crossed the threshold of the Underworld, he spun around. The soul of Eurydice *was* there, hovering in the darkness of the cave behind him. But he had turned too soon. While he stood in the light, she had not yet crossed into the world of the living.

Eurydice began to fade back into the darkness. Orpheus lunged for her, but his arms caught only air. Her sad eyes locked onto his, and she uttered one final word before fading away, "Farewell."

Orpheus approached the entrance to the Underworld once again, singing the same song as before, but this time the way was shut. His music had been mighty enough to move death once, but it could not move it again. Finally, Orpheus went away, heartbroken and alone.

Phaethon and the Chariot of the Sun

Phaethon would have been a happy boy, but the other children his age teased him because he did not know his father. So one day he asked his mother, Clymene, "Who is my father? Do I even have one?" Clymene told Phaethon a secret: He did have a father—a powerful one—but one so busy that Phaethon had never seen him before. Phaethon's father was Helios, the sun god himself. "Every day he drives his shining chariot across the sky," Clymene told him. "That is why he cannot be with us. If he did not do his job, there would be no light to shine upon the earth!"

Phaethon told this to the other children, but they only laughed at him. They did not believe that the sun god was truly his father. "Fine!" Phaethon said. "I will prove it to you!"

He knew the palace of Helios lay on the far eastern edge of the world, where the sun begins its journey every morning. In spite of his mother's protests, he decided to set out on a journey there. "I must go find my father," he said. "Then the whole world will know." He walked for days, and finally he reached the magnificent, shining palace of the sun.

When he entered, a long hallway spread out before him. Along either side stood the Days, the Hours, and the Years—waiting for their time to pass. At the very end, he saw his father seated on his shining throne.

Shocked to see his mortal son, Helios removed his glowing crown, and Phaethon looked upon the face of his father for the first time. "My son!" Helios cried happily. "After all these years, we are finally together." Father and son talked for hours, but at last Phaethon grew brave enough to ask, "Father, would you grant me one request?"

"Anything! You are my son," Helios said happily. "I will promise you whatever you wish! I swear it by the river Styx." This was a foolish choice, for when a god swears on the river Styx, he cannot break his promise.

"Let me drive your golden chariot," said Phaethon. "No one back home believes that you are my father. If my friends see me driving your chariot, I will prove it!"

"Oh no, son," said Helios. "That is far too dangerous!"

"You don't understand," said Phaethon. "They tease me and mock me!"

"Then they are not your friends. You have nothing to prove to them. Besides, the sky-road is so steep that I can barely navigate it. Along the way there are animal-like constellations—the bull, the lion, the scorpion, and the crab—that try to wreck my chariot day after day. Not even Zeus himself could do what I do, and you are just a mortal boy."

Although Helios told Phaethon of each and every danger that lay before him, Phaethon would not listen. He was already imagining himself performing a task that even Zeus himself could not do. He pictured the faces of those who had teased him going pale with astonishment. "I must drive your chariot," said Phaethon resolutely. "I must!"

Helios could not refuse his son. "Very well," he said, defeated. He led Phaethon to where his chariot was kept.

Dawn was nearing. The fiery horses were pawing the ground with anticipation, and Phaethon jumped gleefully into the chariot. Helios shed tears as he smeared protective ointment on his son's body and placed the glowing crown on his head. "Please, son! Take my advice—not my chariot. I do not want to lose you so soon after meeting you!"

"I can do it! I will prove it to you—to everyone!" said Phaethon. "Goodbye, Father!"

The goddess of the dawn threw open the palace doors. Phaethon whipped the fiery horses into motion and the chariot roared up into the sky. Helios watched his departure sadly. "Goodbye, my son."

In only a few seconds the sun chariot soared above the clouds, but by that time, Phaethon was no longer in control of the horses. They sensed that it was a mortal rather than a god holding the reins and began to run amok, taking the sun far off course. Out of the dark regions of the sky lunged fearsome beasts with starry bodies—slashing, biting, and pinching at Phaethon as he flew by. The chariot flew too high and bumped the sky. Then it swooped too low—scorching the land and causing the oceans to boil.

"Wait! Please! I've learned my lesson!" Phaethon cried. "I no longer want to drive the chariot!" But it was too late. The chariot could not be stopped.

The gods on Mount Olympus saw that the earth would be destroyed if something was not done. Reluctantly, Zeus took aim at Phaethon's chariot with one of his thunderbolts.

With a single lightning strike, the chariot was destroyed. The flaming horses ran free like fireflies in the night, and Phaethon fell to the earth, flickering like a falling star.

Helios refused to shine for a day, and darkness covered the earth. Now the world knew the truth about Phaethon's father, but the boy was gone forever.

Atalanta, the Warrior Princess

King Iasus eagerly awaited the birth of his first child. Even though he was growing older, he had never been a father, and this baby was to be his heir—the child to whom his kingdom would be left. But upon receiving word that his wife had given birth to a daughter, instead of the son he so desperately desired, he did the unthinkable: He ordered that the child be left alone in the wilderness to die. "No girl shall inherit my kingdom," he declared.

The baby was abandoned on a fir-covered mountain slope. She would have soon died of cold if a bear, mourning the recent loss of her cub, had not passed by. The human child stirred something inside the beast. The bear licked the dirt from the baby's face and carried her back to her den—intending to raise the child as her own.

While the bear was away from her den, a band of hunters discovered the baby there, cooing and smiling. "A human child?" they said in shock. "We must take her to live with us." As the little girl, who they named **Atalanta**, grew up, she learned the hunters' ways—hunting and trapping to survive—and soon became the best among them. She could outrun any of the other hunters, and her skill with bow and spear was unparalleled.

It was not long after Atalanta had grown into a young woman that she was hunting alone and happened upon a pair of **centaurs**, wild and dangerous creatures with the top half of a man and the hindquarters of a horse. "What do we have here?" they asked, chuckling. "A pretty girl who has lost her way!" Rearing up on their hind legs, they charged Atalanta. But the centaurs underestimated her. Two swift arrows from her bow ended their lives. When the other hunters arrived, they stared in amazement at the slain centaurs, and news of the mighty huntress spread around the countryside.

One day, a young prince accompanied by a band of warriors rode into Atalanta's hunting camp. The prince's name was **Meleager**, and his homeland, **Calydon**, was being ravaged by a supernatural beast—a giant boar with blood-red eyes and tusks as large as an elephant's. It had been sent by the goddess Artemis to punish the people of Calydon for failing to worship her properly.

"Which of you hunters will be brave enough to help me battle this beast?" Meleager asked.

Atalanta readily volunteered. "I will—if you are not threatened by the idea of a woman fighting alongside you."

"Not in the least," replied Meleager, smiling. Atalanta returned with the prince and joined his company of mighty warriors. At first, some of the others were not happy at the thought of a woman joining their ranks. "What is she doing here?" they said. "Hunting is for men!"

Atalanta stared at them undaunted. "I think you will find I am your equal—or dare I say, your better?"

They still protested, but Prince Meleager would not hear of it. "Atalanta has as much right to be here as the rest of us!"

The warriors rode north into the Calydonian wilderness, ready to face the boar's supernatural assault. They tracked its enormous footprints for miles through the forest until Atalanta, catching a strange scent on the wind, cautioned the warriors to stop. "It is here!" she cried.

Roaring like thunder, the boar came crashing through the trees. With its bristles sharp as spears, it tore through the warriors' ranks. Bodies flew through the air as the boar's tusks flung them like rag dolls.

"Face me, pig!" cried Atalanta. The beast turned toward her, its eyes flashing lightning, and charged forward. Boldly standing her ground, Atalanta drew her bow and let a shaft fly. The arrow hit home; the boar squealed and stumbled to the ground only feet before her. Meleager was there in a flash and drove his sword deep into the beast's heart.

As Atalanta and the prince stood victorious, the warriors rushed forward to congratulate Meleager on his kill. "No!" he said. "It is not I who has won honor this day. It is Atalanta."

Atalanta smiled and nodded in recognition of this tribute.

This was only the first of Atalanta's adventures. She went on to do many more mighty deeds—even sailing with Jason and the Argonauts in search of the **Golden Fleece**. In the end, she proved herself one of Greece's greatest heroes.

Perseus and the Quest for Medusa's Head

edusa was a **gorgon**, a monster with live snakes for hair. The sight of her was so frightening that anyone who met her gaze turned into stone. She lived at the edge of the earth with her two gorgon sisters. Anyone foolish enough to journey there did not return. Stories of Medusa's deadly power spread throughout the world, and many brave warriors dreamed of defeating her.

Word of her powers reached the island of **Seriphos**, where a young man named **Perseus** lived with his single mother, **Danaë**. Perseus

loved his mother dearly. But one day, **Polydectes**, the wicked king of Seriphos, carried Danaë away to his palace to be his wife. Although no one was powerful enough to oppose the king, Perseus was determined to save his mother. He addressed the king before all his nobles. "I will journey to the ends of the earth, return with Medusa's head, and use it to defeat you!" The king chuckled. This was even better than he had planned. He had gotten Perseus's mother, and now he was getting rid of her son for good. No one could defeat Medusa—especially not a boy. But unbeknownst to him, two gods had over-heard Perseus's bold claim.

As Perseus sat outside the king's palace, wonder-ing how he could complete such an impossible quest, Athena, the goddess of wisdom, and Hermes, the messenger of the gods, appeared before him. "We have come to aid you," said Athena. In her hands, she carried a sword and a shining shield, one whose surface was as reflective as glass. "No one can look upon Medusa and live," she said, "But her reflection causes no harm." Hermes presented Perseus with a pair of winged sandals, a cap of invisibility, and a satchel that would grow and shrink to fit any object. "Medusa has been causing death and destruction for many years," said Athena. "Use these gifts to end her life once and for all."

Bidding his benefactors thanks and farewell, Perseus used his winged sandals to fly toward the land of Medusa. When the landscape became gray and barren, he knew he must be close. Then he saw the high mountain cave where the gorgon and her sisters were said to live. Surrounding the cave were statues that had once been living beings. Placing his cap of invisibility on his head, Perseus landed before the cave and stepped into its darkness. Even invisible, he was still in danger. The sound of his footsteps could alert the gorgons to his presence, and although Medusa's sisters did not have the same stone-gaze she did, they had tusks and claws that could rip him apart.

Perseus was careful to only look at his shield—he knew one stray glance could cost him his life. Suddenly he saw the reflection of the three sisters. They were sleeping, and Medusa lay in the middle—her eyes closed and her snake hair writhing. He drew his sword to strike, but as he did, the demonic eyes of Medusa opened. Perseus's sword flashed through the air, and Medusa's head fell to the ground. As he grabbed up the head, the snake hair still twisted and bit at his hand.

The sound of Medusa's death had awoken her sisters. They roared and lunged toward the spot where they had seen her head disappear. But Perseus was already gone, flying away on his winged sandals, with the head of Medusa safely in his satchel.

As Perseus headed back home, flying low over the sea, he saw a strange sight. A girl was chained to a rock in the middle of the ocean. Perseus swooped low, removed his cap, and offered his assistance. "Please! Hurry!" she cried. "A sea serpent is coming for me!" The girl, whose name was Andromeda, quickly explained that her parents had offended the spirits of the sea, who in turn had demanded their daughter as a sacrifice. Perseus freed the girl, but before he could carry her away, the enormous sea serpent rose from the waves, opening its jaws to strike. Perseus flew into motion, slicing at the creature with his sword and ending its life. Then Perseus flew on toward home with Andromeda in his arms.

When Perseus returned to Seriphos, he went at once to the banqueting hall of the king, who was stunned to see Perseus alive. "I have returned with what I promised," declared Perseus. The king opened his mouth to object but stopped mid-speech as Perseus held aloft the head of Medusa. The king and all his court had turned to stone.

Perseus was happily reunited with his mother, who welcomed Andromeda into their family with open arms. Athena and Hermes appeared to con-gratulate the young hero, and Athena took the head of Medusa and placed it on her shield. To this day, it still stares forth from her mighty armor.

Pegasus, the Winged Horse

 Echidna was the mother of all monsters, a half-human, half-snake creature who killed anyone unfortunate enough to meet her. A nightmare herself, she gave birth to other nightmares. But her most dreaded child was the **Chimera**, a monster with two heads, one of a lion and one of a goat, and a living serpent for a tail. The Chimera could breathe fire, and she set the countryside for miles around ablaze with her rage. At last Echidna had birthed a monster that would be unstoppable, or so it seemed.

But after the hero Perseus beheaded the snake-haired monster Medusa, something miraculous happened. As Medusa's monstrous blood pooled upon the ground, a creature pure and wonderful came flying forth from it—a winged horse named Pegasus. A monster had given birth to a blessing, one that would bring about the downfall of the Chimera.

For years Pegasus lived wild and free, flying wherever he wished, but finally, a human discovered the secret of taming him. As Pegasus drank from the spring of **Pirene,** his favorite watering hole, he saw a young man timidly approaching him. Normally, the horse winged himself away at the first sight of mortals, but something was glimmering in this human's hand, and it mesmerized Pegasus.

Unbeknownst to the horse, this young man was a would-be hero named **Bellerophon**, who had gone to Athena, the goddess of wisdom, to beg her assistance. In answer to his prayer, she had given him a magical bridle, crafted with her skill and wisdom. Now the clever magic of Athena overpowered Pegasus, and he did not resist as Bellerophon pulled the bridle over his head. The boy sprang up onto Pegasus's back, and horse and rider took to the sky.

On the back of Pegasus, Bellerophon went on many adventures. Athena had foreseen that the boy would need the talents of Pegasus to succeed, and she was right. Bellerophon achieved victory after victory—thanks to the skill of his steed. But never once did he give Pegasus the credit he deserved. Bellerophon became such a sensation that he stirred up his fair share of jealousy. An envious king schemed to end his life by challenging him to slay Greece's foremost monster: the Chimera. Bellerophon accepted. Eager to prove his heroic worth, he turned Pegasus toward the home of the monster.

Over the years, the Chimera had become even deadlier, and the landscape around her lair was now a charred wasteland. She could see far in any direction, and no warrior could approach her on foot. But she had not counted on one approaching from the air.

When the Chimera saw Bellerophon and Pegasus descending from the sky, her snake tail spewed venom, her goat head bleated, and her lion head roared out in anger. She sent a column of flame blazing out to consume them. Pegasus dodged swiftly, aiming his rider toward the monster. Bellerophon drew his bow and sent a rain of arrows down upon the Chimera, but the monster simply burned these up with another blast of her breath. Bellerophon saw her fiery breath must somehow be quenched, and he quickly devised a plan.

Bellerophon attached a lump of lead onto the end of a long spear, and Pegasus swooped low over the beast. As the steed weaved between bursts of fire, Bellerophon hurled the spear into the creature's lion-mouth. The lump of lead lodged in the Chimera's throat, and her fiery breath melted the lead, sealing her throat shut and suffocating her. The Chimera fell lifeless to the ground.

Bellerophon returned victorious, and all of Greece sang his praises. But he was not a true hero, because the fame went right to his head. He seemed to forget the magical horse that had made it all possible. He began to think he deserved a place among the immortals.

There was only one problem: The gods had not offered him such an honor. Foolish Bellerophon decided he would take it for himself. He urged Pegasus toward the top of Mount Olympus. Fortunately, Pegasus was wiser than Bellerophon. As they flew higher and higher, the horse knew something must be done. Zeus would never allow a mortal to approach his palace uninvited, and each thrust of the horse's wings was bringing them closer and closer to their destruction. So before they met such a fate, Pegasus decided to rid himself of his foolish rider. He bucked wildly—flinging Bellerophon off his back. The would-be hero fell all the way down to earth. The fall did not kill him, but it left him broken for the rest of his days.

As for Pegasus, Zeus called him to Olympus, giving him a stable there and the honor of transporting his thunderbolts. Eventually, he placed the winged horse's image in the stars to be remembered forever. In the end it was Pegasus who attained the glory that Bellerophon had so desperately desired.

Hercules Faces the Hydra

nce **Hercules** had been the toast of Greece, the greatest hero ever born. But then his fiercest enemy, the goddess Hera, tricked him into committing a horrible crime without his knowledge. Criminals, even unintentional ones, must pay the penalty. To atone for his crime, the gods demanded Hercules complete **Twelve Labors**, seemingly impossible feats that Hera had personally designed to destroy him. But Hercules was determined to prove her wrong.

This led Hercules to one of his most famous battles. It began with the great hero standing waist deep in a swamp. Here and there little

mossy islands rose from the water, and mist filled the air. **Iolaus**, Hercules's nephew and adventuring companion, held his torch up higher, hoping to penetrate the gloom. "Do you see anything yet?"

"Nothing yet," murmured Hercules.

Over his head and shoulders Hercules wore the skin of a lion, the trophy he had won from the first of his Twelve Labors. The first task had been to slay the Nemean Lion, whose skin no weapon could pierce. But Hercules had simply choked the lion to death, used one of its own claws to skin it, and from then on, wore its impervious hide as a cloak. Now Hercules was after the deadly **Hydra**, whose home was deep in this swamp.

"What do you think the Hydra looks like?" asked Iolaus hesitantly. "A snake?"

"Let's hope not," said Hercules.

Hercules did not like snakes. Hera, who hated him right from the beginning, had tried to end his life when he was just a baby by sending a pair of venomous snakes in to kill him in his cradle. The next morning, when Hercules's mother came to wake him, she found him shaking the dead snakes like a couple of rattles. He had never cared much for snakes ever since.

"No one knows what the Hydra looks like," Hercules said, "because no one lives long enough to find out."

"Whatever it is, it should be no problem for you," said Iolaus.

"Wait a moment," said Hercules. "Look! There!" A half-submerged nest of fallen trees had appeared through the gloom—a black opening yawning wide in its center. "That will be its lair. Bring your torch closer." Hercules climbed onto an island and helped Iolaus up. He pulled an arrow from his quiver, wrapped a bit of cloth around its tip, and lit it upon the boy's torch. "We will let the monster know we are here." Using his mighty bow, he fired the flaming shaft into the nest opening. All was silent for a moment. "Be ready," said Hercules, drawing his sword.

Then, in an explosion of spray, something large broke the surface. Nine heads, sharp-toothed and gnashing, lifted into the air on long serpentine necks. The Hydra locked its eighteen yellow eyes onto Hercules. Then it struck.

One of the heads went for Hercules's sword arm, but he dodged to the side and sliced. The head fell lifeless into the swamp, and the Hydra howled with pain. But immediately the neck stump throbbed with life, and to Hercules's shock, two more heads came shooting out—snapping just as fiercely.

Hercules let loose in a flurry of motion. He throttled and dodged and sliced to defend himself from the snapping and biting of the Hydra heads. But whenever he severed a head, two more heads sprang out just as before. The hero was lost in a writhing mass of Hydra heads. If it had not been for the protection of the lion pelt, the monster's teeth would have shredded him. Hercules knew he must do something—and fast.

"Iolaus, bring your torch!" cried Hercules.

The boy came bravely to his uncle's side. "Do exactly as I say," called Hercules, slicing one of the heads loose. The neck stump began to bubble—two new heads were ready to thrust their way through. "Sear the stump with the torch! Now!" Iolaus did so, and the fire sealed the new heads inside.

"That's it!" yelled Hercules triumphantly, sending his sword through the air. Each time he sliced a head loose, Iolaus seared the stump. They trimmed the Hydra's heads down one by one, until a single head remained.

"Now, beast! You are beaten!" Hercules swung to slice through the final neck, but to his shock, his sword shattered against it. He did not know it, but there was one head of the Hydra that was invincible. This final head rose to strike.

Hercules lifted a huge boulder. "We'll do this a different way." As the Hydra struck, he smashed its final head beneath the boulder. The monster's body thrashed wildly, then slowly grew still.

"See?" he said, leaning upon the boulder and breathing heavily. "Nothing to it." He clapped a brawny hand on Iolaus's shoulder. "Thank you! I could not have done it without you! Two down. Ten to go."

Before they left the swamp, Hercules dipped each of his arrows in the Hydra's poisonous blood. Just like the lion's pelt, these would be another mighty weapon to aid him in the rest of his Twelve Labors.

Ariadne
in the Labyrinth

Princess **Ariadne** knew her father, King **Minos** of Crete, was a stern man. But she did not know how truly cruel he was until she discovered his secret: Beneath the floors of their palace was a sprawling maze called the Labyrinth. Inside that maze roamed a monster called the **Minotaur**—half-man, half-bull. Lying awake at night, she could hear its shuffling hooves and its eerie bellowing in the passageways beneath her.

Soon after Ariadne had made this discovery, a black-sailed ship arrived in the Cretan harbor. Aboard was a group of boys and girls from the city-state of Athens, across the sea.

The Athenians had angered Minos years earlier when his son had died competing in a sports contest in their city-state. Every seven years since then he demanded a sacrifice—seven boys and seven girls. The guards led these prisoners into the palace to appear before Ariadne's father. Their hands were bound, and their faces were stained with tears. "Sons and daughters of Athens," Minos growled. "Tonight you will be given to my monster. Your deaths will buy seven more years of peace for your homeland." The guards led the young prisoners to the entrance of the Labyrinth and forced them inside. The Athenian prisoners beat upon the gate, but they could not escape. They fled into the darkness and were soon lost in the Labyrinth's twisting passageways. The Minotaur found them soon enough, and their dying cries echoed beneath the palace. They haunted Ariadne's dreams for many years to come.

"I must escape this place," said Ariadne to herself, "no matter what the cost."

Seven years passed. The black-sailed ship arrived again. This time Ariadne was older, and she had given up hope of ever escaping Crete. As the Athenian captives, almost her same age, were led before Minos, Ariadne noticed a bold young man among them. There was something different about him. He did not lower his head like the others but stood with the bearing of the king.

Ariadne did not know it, but this was **Theseus**, the son of King **Aegeus** of Athens. Against his father's protests, he had volunteered to come to Crete to end the sacrifices once and for all. Something told Ariadne this young man was her chance to escape. He could brave the Labyrinth and defeat the Minotaur. But he could not do it alone.

The Labyrinth had been built by the master craftsman **Daedalus**, who still lived in Minos's palace. Ariadne went to him to ask how the maze might be beaten.

Daedalus himself was from Athens. He, too, wanted to end the sacrifices, so he told Ariadne the Labyrinth's secret.

"All the passageways lead to the center of the maze," said Daedalus. "But once you have reached the center, it is almost impossible to find your way back again. The only way to enter the Labyrinth and come out again is to tie one end of a spool of thread to the entrance. Then follow it back to its beginning." The princess thanked the inventor for his bravery.

Ariadne found a spool of golden thread and snuck down to where the prisoners were kept. All were asleep except for Theseus. His clear eyes peered out through the darkness. When he saw her, he looked up in surprise.

"I know you are surprised to see me here," whispered Ariadne. "I have come to release you. You must face the Minotaur tonight, and I will help you defeat him."

"You are Minos's daughter. Why are you doing this?" asked Theseus.

"To help you—to stop these deaths," said Ariadne. "All I ask is that you take me with you when you escape."

"I promise," said Theseus.

Ariadne led Theseus to the secret entrance of the Labyrinth and placed the golden thread into his hand. She told him everything Daedalus had told her, and then Theseus disappeared into the darkness. For a moment, Ariadne held the spool in her hand, watching it unwind, but her curiosity was too great. She tied the end of the spool to the entrance of the Labyrinth and followed the trail of golden thread through the darkness.

Before she reached the heart of the Labyrinth, she heard the sounds of a struggle and hurried forward. In the maze's central chamber, Theseus was wrestling the Minotaur. The sight of the creature was like a nightmare—it had a muscular human torso topped by a bull's head. It flung Theseus away, lowered its horns, and charged. Theseus dodged to the side, grabbed a fallen sword, and dealt the monster his death stroke. Theseus stood and surveyed his handiwork, declaring, "The monster is dead."

The rest seemed like a dream to Ariadne. They followed the golden thread back to the Labyrinth's entrance, freed the other prisoners, boarded the black-sailed ship, and sailed toward Athens. She was finally free.

Daedalus and Icarus

Daedalus was known throughout Greece as the greatest inventor to ever live. He had made many marvelous inventions—works that even rivaled the works of the gods. He invented the first sail and crafted statues so lifelike they seemed to breathe and move.

It was no surprise when King Minos of Crete had invited Daedalus to his island kingdom for a special project—building the Labyrinth, a twisting maze to hold the Minotaur.

Daedalus designed the Labyrinth to perfection. No one could escape it without the inventor's help. So when Theseus of Athens was able to navigate the Labyrinth and defeat the Minotaur, King Minos knew Daedalus had helped him.

"You dare betray me?" bellowed Minos. "For that, you will never leave Crete!" It seemed Daedalus and his young son, **Icarus**, would be trapped there forever.

After this, Daedalus went to a cliff near his workshop every day and stared out over the sea. In spite of all his genius, he could not escape.

One day as Daedalus and Icarus were standing on the cliff, watching the seagulls wheel in the breeze, Icarus asked, "Why can't we just fly away—like the birds?"

"That's it!" gasped Daedalus. "Quick, Icarus! Back to our workshop!"

Daedalus began to sketch furiously and then laughed to himself. "Yes! It could work! But we'll need feathers. Many feathers!"

He made two small snares out of rope and found some crumbs to bait them with. Then he and Icarus set their traps near the sea cliff.

"We'll catch a bag full of gulls and use their feathers to make our escape," said Daedalus.

When they had filled a bag with seagulls, Daedalus carried it back to their workshop. He worked all night fashioning wooden frames that resembled the wings of birds. Using melted wax, he attached the gulls' feathers to the frames. Then Daedalus built two leather harnesses and attached his newly made wings to these. The next morning, he appeared before Icarus with a pair of white wings upon his shoulders.

"Are you going to fly?" asked Icarus, excited.

"We both will." Daedalus smiled and helped Icarus attach his own smaller set of wings. "But first, we need a test." They took their wings to the cliffside. Daedalus paced backward from the cliff's edge. Then, with great speed, he ran forward and jumped out onto the breeze.

At first he fell, but the wind caught him up and carried him into the sky. He looped back over Icarus's head, and with several settling flaps, landed neatly in front of his son.

"My turn!" cried Icarus, running for the cliff.

"No, son!" said Daedalus, catching Icarus. "Don't rush ahead foolishly before thinking. There are things I must tell you first. Always fly straight over the water. If you fly too close to the ocean's spray, your feathers will get wet. They will grow too heavy, and you will fall into the ocean and drown. If you fly too high, the heat of the sun will melt the wax that holds the wings together. Please, fly at a moderate height, or you will be in great danger."

"I know what to do," Icarus said, scowling. "I watched you do it!"

"Promise me, Icarus," said Daedalus.

The boy promised, and the inventor wrapped his winged arms around his son.

Soon father and son were soaring on the salty sea breeze. The sensation of flying thrilled Icarus.

"Father! This is greater than I imagined!" cried Icarus. "I feel like one of the gods!"

Icarus made great loops in the sky.

Over the wind, Daedalus shouted, "Icarus, be careful! This isn't a game! You promised!"

"What? I can't hear you! Hurry up, Father. I'll beat you there if you're not careful!"

The inventor beat his wings furiously to catch up with his son, but Icarus easily outpaced him.

"Icarus!" he called. "You're flying too fast—and too high!"

Icarus looked back over his shoulder. His father was far below him. Then the boy looked up. The sun was much too close. Its heat was bearing down upon him.

Something hot and sticky was running down both his arms. He flapped them furiously to shake it off, but when he did, feathers flew loose in all

directions. To his
horror, Icarus
began to fall.

"No! Father,
help me!" he cried.

Daedalus saw
his son spiraling
down toward
the sea, a trail of
feathers behind
him. He turned

his head away just before Icarus crashed into
the ocean.

"Icarus. Icarus," he wept. "My son, why did you
not listen?"

Time and time again, the old man swooped as low
as he dared over the spot where his son had fallen,
yet he never saw any trace of the boy. Finally, he
gave up hope and, despairing, continued his flight
toward Greece.

Many sailors later reported seeing a large bird in
the sky that day, a bird with its head hung low. They
said it had the strangest cry—like a man whose
heart was breaking.

The Fate of Achilles

Thetis the sea nymph knew her son, Achilles, was destined for greatness— and that was what worried her. A prophecy foretold that he would be a great warrior, but if he went to war, he would die young.

Thetis was immortal, so she took her darling boy to the river Styx in the Underworld. Any mortal who bathed in the river Styx would become impervious to harm. So Thetis took Achilles by the heel and dipped him into those mystical waters. But she forgot to dip the heel by which she held him, unintentionally leaving Achilles with one spot of vulnerability.

Growing up in Greece, Achilles dreamed of being a great warrior, much to his mother's

dismay. He longed for a chance to prove his skill, and that chance came when the kings of Greece declared war on **Troy**, a city-state across the sea in **Anatolia**.

It all started with an argument between three of the most powerful goddesses, Hera, Athena, and Aphrodite, over who was the most beautiful. They first asked Zeus to judge between them, but when he wisely refused, he suggested that Paris, a young prince of Troy, should be their unbiased judge. Paris agreed to judge the goddesses, but each goddess tried to sway him by offering him a secret bribe. Hera offered him power, Athena offered him fighting ability, and Aphrodite offered him love—the love of the Greek queen, Helen of Sparta, the most beautiful woman in the world.

Paris chose love.

Aphrodite sent Paris to the Greek city-state of **Sparta**, where he courted Helen and took her back to Troy. Many of the kings of Greece had sworn an oath to protect Helen, so they declared war on Troy, vowing to sail across the sea and retrieve her.

Terrified, Thetis went to Achilles. "Don't go to war, my son! If you stay here in Greece, it's true that you will never win fame and renown, but you will live a long, happy life. If you go to Troy, you will gain glory, but you will die before your time."

Achilles chose glory.

Greece had never seen a war like this. Nearly every king and warrior in Greece was armed and ready to fight. A thousand ships filled with soldiers sailed to Troy, and the Greeks surrounded the enemy city. They thought Troy would fall quickly.

But Troy was surrounded by thick walls built by the gods Poseidon and Apollo, and the Trojan people were valiant warriors. Their war leader, the noble Prince **Hector**, was ready to defend his brother, Paris, against the invading Greeks.

Frantic to protect her son, Thetis asked Hephaestus, the god of the forge, to make special armor for Achilles. Although Achilles was protected by the power of the river Styx, she was still worried about the prophecy. Fitted with his new armor, Achilles became an even more fearsome foe. Enemy warriors bolted at the sight of him, and those foolish enough to face him paid with their lives.

The Greek army was massive, but the Trojans summoned mighty allies. Prince Memnon of **Ethiopia**, a land far to the south, came to aid Troy with his army of dark-skinned warriors. Memnon was a skilled fighter, said to be the son of Eos, the goddess of the dawn. He and his warriors pushed the Greeks back, but when Prince Memnon came face-to-face with Achilles, he was defeated. At his death, he and his soldiers turned into birds and flew away.

Then came the powerful **Amazon** queen, Penthesilea, who brought her army of warrior women to fight for Troy. The Amazons were the daughters of **Ares**, the god of war, and absolutely no men were allowed in their tribe. Penthesilea and her warriors fought fearlessly, but she, too, fell to Achilles in battle.

For nine long years, Achilles helped lead the Greek warriors against the Trojans, but they could never break through the city's walls.

The Trojans worshipped the same gods as the Greeks, and the gods of Olympus had been split by the conflict. Apollo, the god of light and truth, favored Troy. He saw that Achilles must fall. Fortunately for him, he had discovered Achilles's weakness—his one unprotected heel. One day as Achilles battled before the walls of Troy, Apollo inspired Paris to fire an arrow toward the warrior. Apollo guided Paris's arrow into Achilles's heel. All of Achilles's weakness was concentrated in that spot, and this made the wound mortal. Mighty Achilles fell. Although he had never been defeated in hand-to-hand combat, he had been defeated all the same.

The war continued—without Achilles. The Greeks finally defeated the Trojans, not by force, but through the trick of the Trojan Horse.

In the end, Achilles achieved his goal. His name did live on after him—heralded as the greatest warrior who ever lived. But his life was more of a tragedy than a triumph. No one could forget that Greece's greatest warrior had been brought down by his heel.

In the Cave of the Cyclops

The ten-year Trojan War had finally come to an end—thanks to the Greek king **Odysseus**. Odysseus had devised the idea of the Trojan Horse, a wooden horse-shaped structure that looked like a sacrifice to the gods but actually held a troop of Greek soldiers. When the Trojans allowed the horse inside the city, the soldiers waited until nightfall. Then they climbed out of the horse, opened the city gates, and took Troy by surprise. So fell Troy.

Now Odysseus and his men were on their way home to his kingdom of **Ithaca**. Along the way, they stopped for supplies on an unknown

island, where an enormous cave opened in the side of a cliff. Inside, Odysseus and his men found empty sheep pens and jars of milk and cheese. They helped themselves to the food and waited for the person who lived there to return. After all, the laws of the gods declared that everyone had to show strangers hospitality.

The men were in for a surprise. The cave dweller was not a human at all, but a towering Cyclops with one blinking eye in the middle of his forehead. As he drove his sheep back into the cave, the Cyclops stared down at the unwelcome humans.

Odysseus approached him boldly. "Greetings, friend," he said. "We are sailing home from Troy. We hope you don't mind, but we helped ourselves to milk and cheese. We were just so hungry." The Cyclops did not reply. Instead he rolled an enormous boulder across the cave entrance.

Then he snatched two of Odysseus's men and devoured them. As the others fled for cover, the Cyclops bellowed, "You will pay me back for what you have stolen! You are trapped in this cave, and I will eat you one by one."

The next morning the Cyclops rolled the boulder away and took his sheep out to graze, but not before catching another man and eating him for breakfast. As he rolled the boulder back into place, he grinned at the men. "See you at dinnertime."

Odysseus devised a plan to escape. First he found a large club that belonged to the Cyclops. Odysseus ordered his men to whittle this down to a sharp point. Then they hid it beneath the sheep dung on the floor and waited.

When the Cyclops returned, Odysseus approached him kindly. "We would like to offer you a gift as our gracious host." He offered the Cyclops some wine, which they had brought with them from Troy.

"This is good!" the Cyclops said, greedily gulping the wine. "I am **Polyphemus**, son of Poseidon. What is your name?"

"My name?" said Odysseus slyly. "My name is Nobody."

"In return for this kind gift," Polyphemus said, "I will eat Nobody last of all."

Then the Cyclops ate another of Odysseus's men and went to sleep. Odysseus commanded his men to uncover the spike they had made. They heated one end of it in the fire and then, hoisting it over their heads, drove it into the eye of the sleeping Cyclops.

Polyphemus awoke in a roar of rage. The men fled from his grasping hands. "Be careful!" Odysseus called. "Even blind, he is still dangerous."

Polyphemus opened the cave entrance and called out to his Cyclops brothers. "Brothers! Help me! I have been blinded! Nobody has blinded me! Nobody has taken my eye!"

Hearing this nonsense, the other Cyclopes thought Polyphemus was just dreaming, and they did not come to his aid.

So Polyphemus sat down before the cave entrance, blocking the way. "None of you will escape! If you try to leave, I will catch you!" he bellowed.

Hours passed. The sheep began to bleat, wanting to graze, and Odysseus saw a way to escape. He tied the sheep together two by two. Then he whispered for his men to cling to the underside of each pair of sheep.

"All right," said Polyphemus said to his sheep. "I will let you graze, but I will feel you as you pass." Polyphemus opened the gate, and as the sheep left the cave, the Cyclops felt of them to make sure they were sheep passing and not men. Hidden beneath the sheep, the men of Odysseus safely passed the Cyclops. The last to depart was Odysseus, riding beneath the ram of the flock.

When they were all free and aboard their ship, Odysseus looked back. Polyphemus was sitting in the cave entrance—still thinking he had them trapped. Odysseus could not resist a boast. "Foolish Cyclops!" he called. "I told you my name was Nobody, but if anyone asks, tell them it was Odysseus who defeated you!"

Hearing this, Polyphemus jumped up and called out to his father, Poseidon, the god of the seas.

"Father Poseidon! Hear my cry!" he said. "Make sure Odysseus never sees his home again!" The seas rumbled a response, and Odysseus realized the foolishness of his actions. It would take ten more years for Odysseus to finally outwit Poseidon and make his way home to Ithaca.

Penelope Outwits Her Suitors

hen Odysseus, King of Ithaca, left for the Trojan War, he promised his wife, **Penelope**, he would return. So Penelope waited patiently. Ten years passed, and word reached Greece that the war had ended. The kings of Greece would be coming home. Although ships returned filled with many husbands, Odysseus did not. Penelope told herself he would be home soon. But ten more years passed. No Odysseus.

Soon people began to say that Odysseus was never coming home. This is when young men from Ithaca and the surrounding isles saw their chance. Over a hundred **suitors**

converged on Penelope's home, all seeking her hand in marriage. What they were truly after was the throne of Ithaca.

"My lady," they said. "Admit it. Your husband is dead."

"Not dead, good sir," she responded. "Only delayed. Odysseus will return. Athena, the goddess of wisdom, watches over him."

So the rude suitors decided to take advantage of Penelope's hospitality. They moved into the hall of Ithaca, eating her food and drinking her wine. They told themselves that soon the gentle queen would give in and take a new husband. But Penelope was tougher than they thought.

Even after months of the suitors living in her home, having her servants wait on them hand and foot, Penelope showed no signs of weakening. "Enough is enough!" the suitors cried. "Choose one of us—any of us! You have no reason not to choose." Penelope saw in the suitors' eyes they meant business. Murder was not beyond them, and her son, **Telemachus**, was nearing the age of manhood. He would soon become their target. She knew she must use her wits to protect herself and her son. "I *will* choose between you," she began, and the suitors' eyes lit up, "when I have finished weaving a burial cloth for my father-in-law, Laertes." The suitors wilted. Laertes, Odysseus's father, was in poor health, and it seemed he would soon die.

Many of the suitors were angry at Penelope's terms, but their leaders calmed them. "Don't worry," they said. "How long can a bit of weaving take?" Once again, they had underestimated Penelope.

Penelope went to work. By day, she toiled tirelessly at her tapestry. In its web of colorful thread, she put the image of the sea and Odysseus's ship tossed upon it. Yet each night, when the household was asleep, Penelope pulled loose the day's threads. Through this trick, the suitors were deceived.

Out of all the servants in Penelope's household, some were still loyal to her, but ten of her handmaids had taken up with the suitors, becoming their spies. One night, one of the handmaidens saw Penelope pulling loose the tapestry's threads and reported this to the suitors.

The next day the leader of the suitors confronted Penelope in front of all the household. "You are no lady!" he sneered. "You have been deceiving us! Now choose one of us—or else!" It seemed she had no choice. It had been nearly twenty years. Perhaps Odysseus was dead.

But there was still fire in her soul, and Penelope faced her suitors defiantly. "I will only marry the man who is the measure of my husband." She called for Odysseus's bow, a weapon so weathered and inflexible that it was nearly impossible to string. "I choose the man who can string Odysseus's bow and shoot an arrow through twelve axe rings."

Twelve axes were driven into the floor with the rings on the ends of their handles lined up in a row. One by one, the suitors tried to bend the inflexible bow and secure the bow-string, but none of them were strong enough to do so. Even Telemachus

tried, but he could not.

"Enough with your tricks!" the suitors cried. "Propose another task! No one can complete this one!"

"I can," said an old beggar man. A few days earlier the old man had arrived in Ithaca, and no one knew from where. The suitors roared in laughter as the beggar hobbled into the midst of the hall and took up the bow. Holding it against his calf, he bent it and looped the arrow string into place. "There's a trick to it, you see," the old man said. Then he rose and fired an arrow neatly through all twelve axe rings.

"What is the meaning of this?" yelled the suitors. "Who is this beggar man?"

Then the beggar's disguise, given to him by Athena, fell away. "I am Odysseus," he said.

With the help of Telemachus, Odysseus repaid the suitors for their rudeness and cleansed Ithaca of its traitors. Those who were not slain fled for their lives.

With the suitors defeated, Odysseus turned to his wife. Penelope's eyes shone with love. "I knew you'd come back to me," she said as the couple embraced for the first time in twenty years. "Welcome home."

Achilles (uh-KILL-eez): The greatest warrior of all time

Aegeus (AY-jus): The king of Athens

Amazons: A race of warrior women

Anatolia (an-uh-TOE-lee-uh): The westernmost part of Asia

Aphrodite (af-ruh-DY-tee): The goddess of love

Apollo (uh-PAH-lo): The god of light, truth, and music

Ares (AIR-eez): The god of war

Ariadne (air-ee-AD-nee): The princess of Crete

Artemis (AR-tuh-mis): The goddess of the hunt and the moon

Atalanta (at-uh-LAN-tuh): A warrior princess

Athena (uh-THEE-nuh): The goddess of wisdom

Attica (AT-ih-kuh): A peninsula in Greece

Bellerophon (buh-LEHR-uh-fun): A would-be hero and tamer of Pegasus

Calliope (kuh-LY-uh-pee): A muse; mother of Orpheus

Calydon (KAH-luh-don): A city-state in mainland Greece

centaur (SIN-tar): A creature with the top half of a human and the hindquarters of a horse

Cerberus (SER-buh-rus): The three-headed guard dog of the Underworld

Charon (KAH-run): The ferryman of the river Styx

Chimera (ky-MEE-ruh): A fire-breathing creature with a head of a lion, a head of a goat, and the tail of a snake

city-state: A city that rules the surrounding territory with the authority of a state

Crete (kreet): The largest of the Greek islands

Cronus (KRO-nus): The leader of the Titans

Cyclopes (sy-KLO-peez): Giant creatures having only one eye each (singular spelling is *Cyclops*, pronounced SY-klopz)

Daedalus (DAY-duh-lus): The greatest inventor to ever live

Danaë (DA-nuh-ee): The mother of the hero Perseus

Delos (DEE-lowz): An island

Delphi (DEL-fy): A city in mainland Greece

Demeter (dih-MEE-tur): The goddess of the harvest

Eros (EH-ros): The god of love

Ethiopia: Not to be confused with the African country, it is a mythical region at the ends of the earth that is home to a dark-skinned race of people

Eurydice (yoo-RID-uh-see): The wife of Orpheus

Gaea (JEE-uh): The mother of the Titans and personification of the earth

gods: The next generation of supernatural beings after the Titans

Golden Fleece: A legendary treasure sought by the hero Jason

gorgon (GOR-gun): A monster with living snakes for hair

Hades (HAY-deez): The Lord of the Underworld

Hector (HEK-ter): A prince of Troy and leader of the Trojan army

Helios (HEE-lee-os): The god of the sun

Hephaestus (huh-FAY-stus): The god of fire and the forge

Hera (HEH-ruh): The queen of the gods

Hercules (HER-kyuh-leez): A hero known for his enormous strength

Hermes (HER-meez): The messenger god

Hestia (HES-tee-uh): The first of the gods, the goddess of the hearth and home

Hydra (HY-druh): A many-headed monster

Icarus (IH-kr-us): The son of Daedalus

Iolaus (eye-oh-LAY-us): The nephew of and companion to Hercules

Ithaca (IH-thuh-kuh): An island off the west coast of mainland Greece

Lemnos (LEM-nos): An island in the Aegean Sea

Leto (LAY-toe): A Titan and the mother of Artemis and Apollo

lyre (LY-r): A small harp

Medusa (mih-DOO-suh): The deadliest of the gorgons

Meleager (muh-LEE-gr): The prince of Calydon

Minos (MY-nos): The king of Crete

Minotaur (MY-no-tar): A creature with the head of a bull and the body of a man

Mount Olympus: The tallest mountain in Greece, said to be the home of the gods

Mount Parnassus: A high mountain in mainland Greece

Narcissus (nar-SIS-us): A handsome man

nymph (nimf): A female nature spirit

Odysseus (o-DIS-ee-us): The king of Ithaca, hero of the Trojan War

oracle: A person who receives divine messages from the gods

Orpheus (OR-fee-us): The most talented musician who ever lived; son of Apollo and Calliope

Penelope (peh-NEL-o-pee): The clever queen of Ithaca

Perseus (PER-see-us): The man who defeated Medusa

Pirene (pih-REE-nee): A spring in Corinth that started flowing when Pegasus pawed the ground there

Polydectes (pol-ee-DEK-teez): The wicked king of Seriphos

Polyphemus (pol-ee-FEE-mus): A Cyclops and son of Poseidon

Poseidon (puh-SY-dun): The god of the sea

priestess: A woman who serves in the temple of a particular god or goddess

prophecy: A prediction of the future

Rhea (REE-uh): The queen of the Titans, the mother of the first gods

Seriphos (SEHR-uh-fus): An island southeast of mainland Greece

Sparta: A city-state in Greece

Styx (stiks): The river that forms the boundary between the earth and the Underworld

suitor: A man who pursues a woman with the intent of marriage

Telemachus (tuh-LEM-uh-kus): The son of Penelope and Odysseus

temple: A building devoted to the worship of a god

Theseus (THEE-see-us): The prince of Athens

Thetis (THEE-tus): A sea nymph, mother of Achilles and the one who raised Hephaestus

Titans: The generation of supernatural beings that existed before the gods

trident: A three-pronged spear

Troy: A city-state in Anatolia

Twelve Labors: A series of tasks intended to punish the hero Hercules

Underworld: The land beneath the earth where all dead souls reside

Zeus (zoos): The king of the gods

Ancient Greece for Kids
greece.mrdonn.org

Learn all about Anicent Greece, including its people, geography, and myths.

Goddess Power: A Kids' Book of Greek and Roman Mythology
by Yung In Chae

From tales of Gaia, Goddess of Earth, to Aphrodite, Goddess of Love and Beauty, these legendary stories are paired with artwork that brings the myths to life.

Greeking Out
kids.nationalgeographic.com/zeus-the-mighty /topic/podcast

This podcast series covers some of the greatest Greek myths ever told.

Introduction to Mythology for Kids: Legendary Stories from around the World
by Zachary Hamby

This collection of mythology for kids takes you from ancient Mesopotamia to the Abenaki tribes of northeastern United States and Canada, showing you myths from around the world.

The Lightning Thief: Percy Jackson and the Olympians, Book 1
by Rick Riordan

The first in a series based on Greek mythology, this fantasy-adventure novel centers on a boy who learns that his father is Poseidon, the Greek god of the sea. Percy sets out on a quest across the United States to stop a war between the gods.

Olympians
by George O'Connor

This 12-book series of graphic novels chronicles the myths of the Greek gods. Drawing from the original versions, these retellings are written and illustrated by O'Connor in comics form.

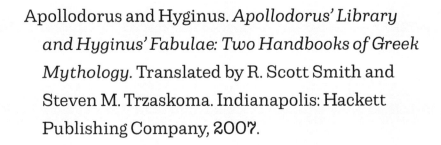

REFERENCES

Apollodorus and Hyginus. *Apollodorus' Library and Hyginus' Fabulae: Two Handbooks of Greek Mythology.* Translated by R. Scott Smith and Steven M. Trzaskoma. Indianapolis: Hackett Publishing Company, 2007.

Hamilton, Edith. *Mythology.* New York: Little, Brown, and Company, 1942.

Homer. *Iliad.* Translated by Robert Fagles. New York: Penguin Books, 1990.

Homer. *Odyssey.* Translated by Robert Fagles. New York: Penguin Books, 1997.

Ovid. *Metamorphoses.* Translated by Charles Martin. New York: W. W. Norton & Company, 2004.

Tripp, Edward. *Crowell's Handbook of Classical Mythology.* New York: Thomas Y. Crowell Company, 1970.

INDEX

U

Z

ACKNOWLEDGMENTS

I would like to thank Callisto Media for this opportunity and my editor, Julie Haverkate, for her expertise and guidance.

I would like to thank my parents, who taught me from an early age to cultivate creativity and use it to better the lives of others.

I am thankful for my children, Luke and Jane, who are my joy.

As always, I would like to thank Rachel—my editor, my supporter, my wife, my friend.

And, most of all, I would like to thank God for giving his creations the power of creation themselves.

ABOUT THE AUTHOR

Zachary Hamby is an English teacher in rural Missouri. He wrote the two series Reaching Olympus and Mythology for Teens as well as *World Mythology for Beginners, Introduction to Mythology for Kids,* and *The Hero's Guidebook.* He resides in the Ozarks with his wife, Rachel (also an English teacher), and their two children, Luke and Jane. For more information about Zachary, visit his website creativeenglishteacher.com or contact him by email at zachary@creativeenglishteacher.com.

ABOUT THE ILLUSTRATOR

Yancey Labat has been illustrating since his elementary school days, when his friends would ask him to draw action heroes for them. He started his career with Marvel Comics and has since illustrated many comic books, children's books, and graphic novels, including the award-winning and *New York Times* bestselling DC Super Hero Girls series.

Printed in the USA
CPSIA information can be obtained
at www.ICGtesting.com
LVHW052226030124
767690LV00006B/72